FRIENDS OF
MINNESOTA BARNS

BARN COLORING BOOK

Dedicated to Barn Lovers Everywhere

FRIENDS OF
MINNESOTA BARNS

FPS LLC

Book design and typesetting by James Monroe Design LLC
Text and Images by: Jim Lammers

26 25 24 23 22   5 4 3 2 1
First Edition

ISBN 13: 978-1-0879-1385-8

Library of Congress data available upon request.

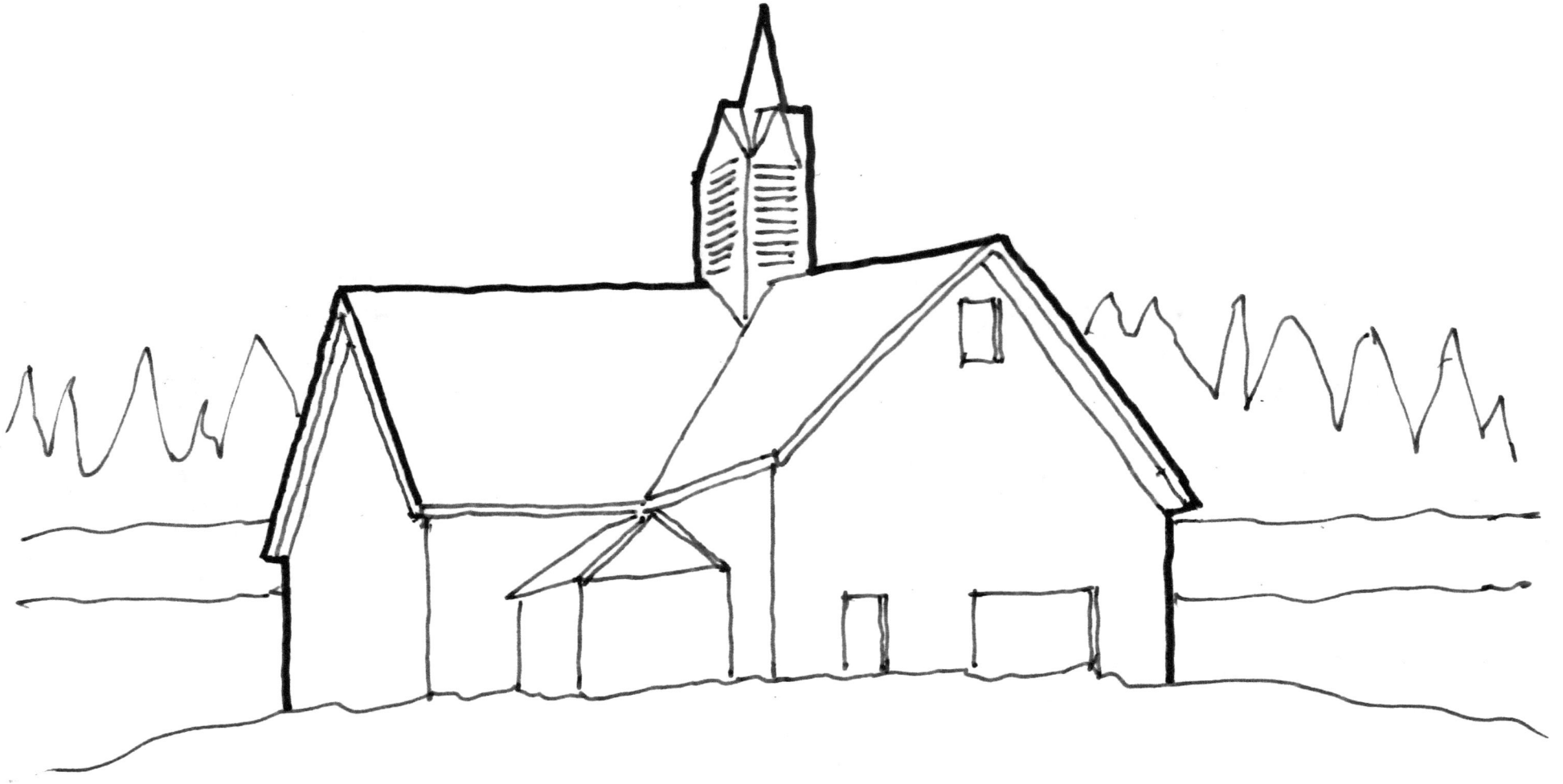

This is a favorite barn. It has a cupola that looks like a church steeple.
It is a simple gable-ended barn located near Stark.

This is a good example of a 'Wisconsin Dairy Barn' near Scandia. It's long and narrow with lots of windows for the cows. The small house that's been added to the barn is a 'Milk House' and it's used to sanitize the milk machine and milk buckets and cans. One of the windows has a hood for a fan to ventilate the milking floor. Cows don't smell all that good.

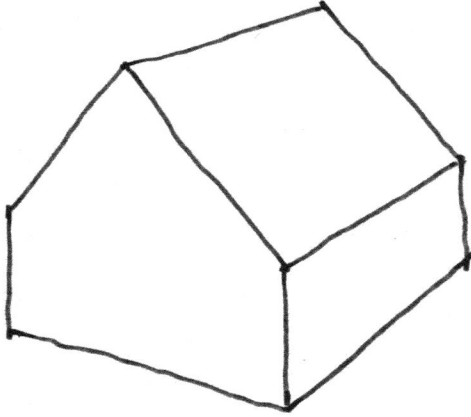

Gable

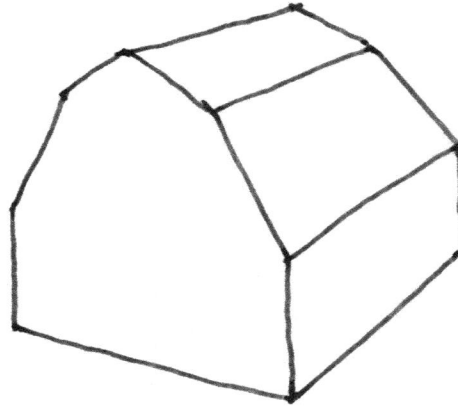

Gambrel

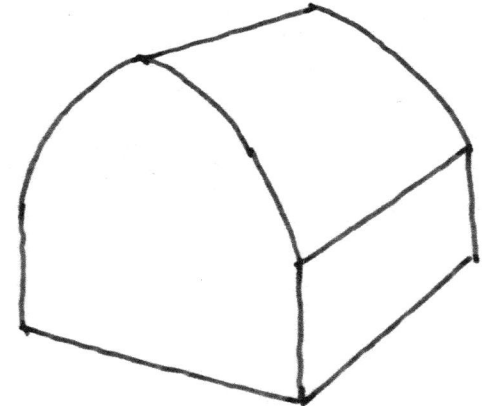

Gothic Arch

The three most common Minnesota barn roof types.

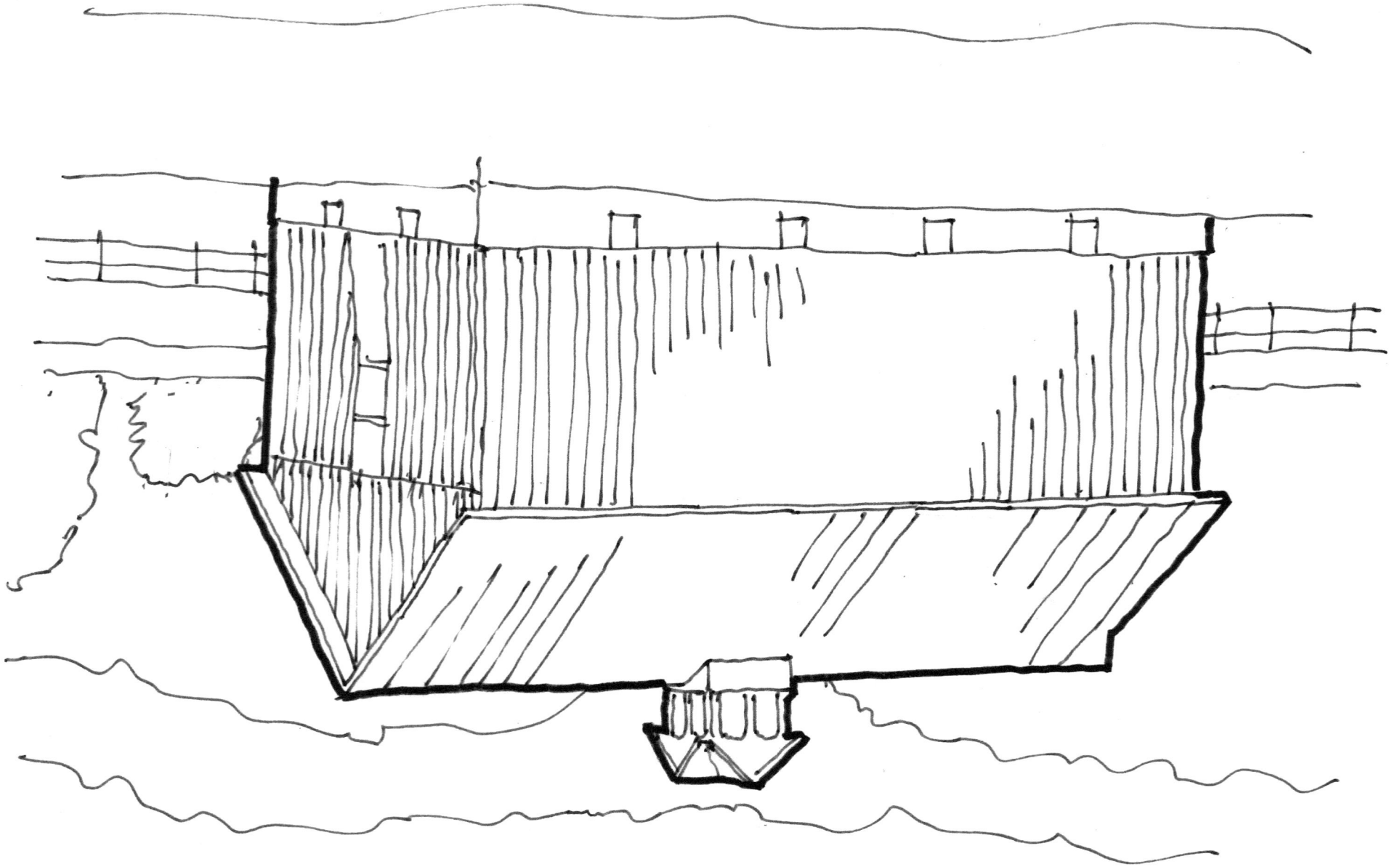

A lovely old gable-ended barn with impressive cupola on top. It's located in Houston County.

Here's a nice old gambrel roofed barn with a fieldstone foundation and horses out front.
It's near Montgomery.

A gambrel-roofed barn with milkhouse attached at the back. Located in Chisago County.

A grouping of farm buildings and an old barn in the middle.

This dairy barn near Stanton has a milk house attached and 'pilasters' or 'buttresses' supporting the stone foundation wall.

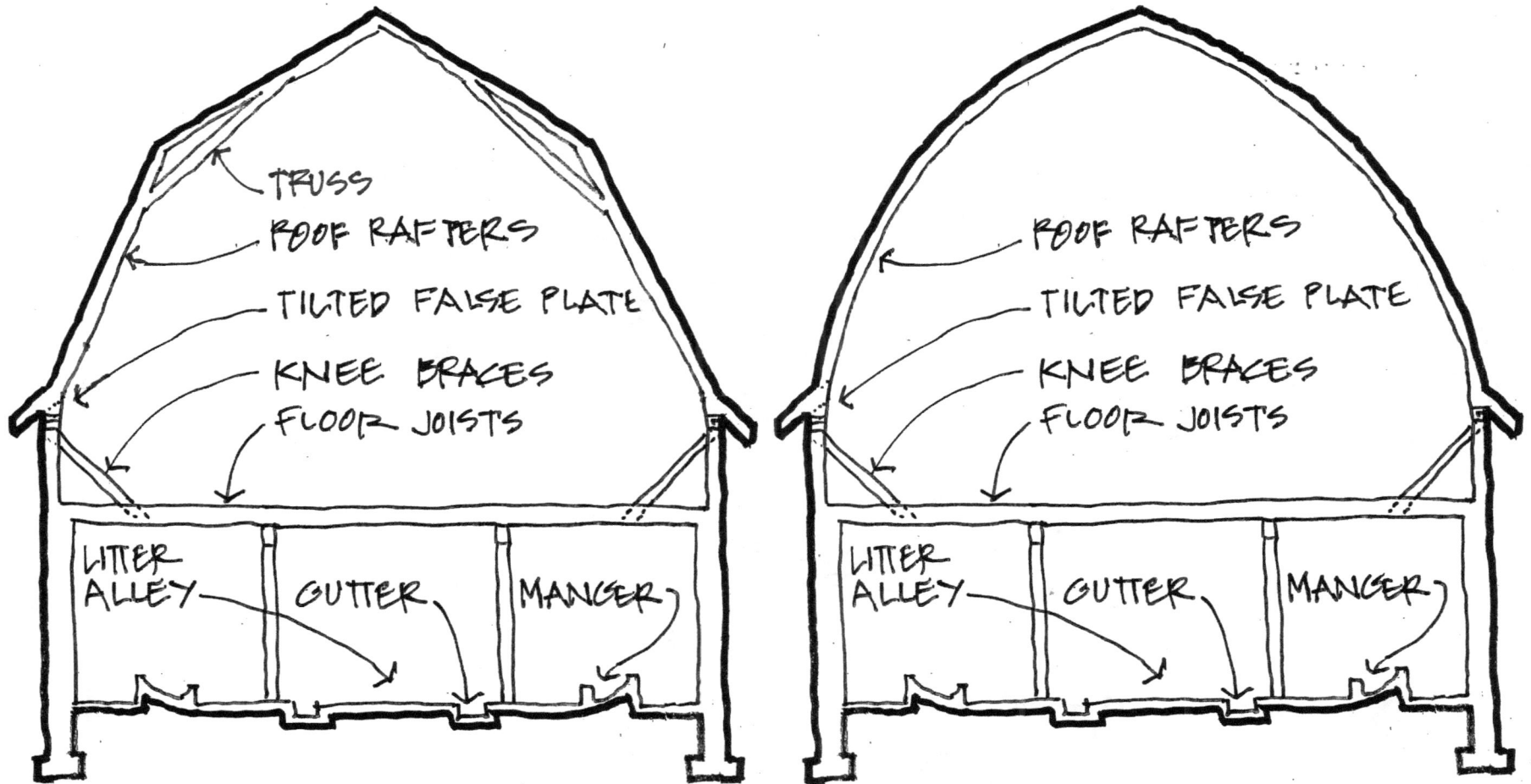

TRUSS
ROOF RAFTERS
TILTED FALSE PLATE
KNEE BRACES
FLOOR JOISTS

LITTER ALLEY
GUTTER
MANGER

ROOF RAFTERS
TILTED FALSE PLATE
KNEE BRACES
FLOOR JOISTS

LITTER ALLEY
GUTTER
MANGER

Here's a comparison of the Gambrel Roof and the Gothic Arch Roof. Can you see the differences?

This gothic arch barn has a really large silo and a tilted false plate. It is near Cross Lake.

This diagram shows a Tilted False Plate which is used to prevent water coming off the roof from running down the side of the barn. It can easily be seen in the drawing of a lovely gothic arch barn with board and batten siding and a granary/milk house addition near Franconia.

This is a corn crib used for storing ears of corn. The boards on the sides and on the ends are spaced apart to let the air circulate to dry out the ears of corn. Later they will be ground up and fed to the animals.

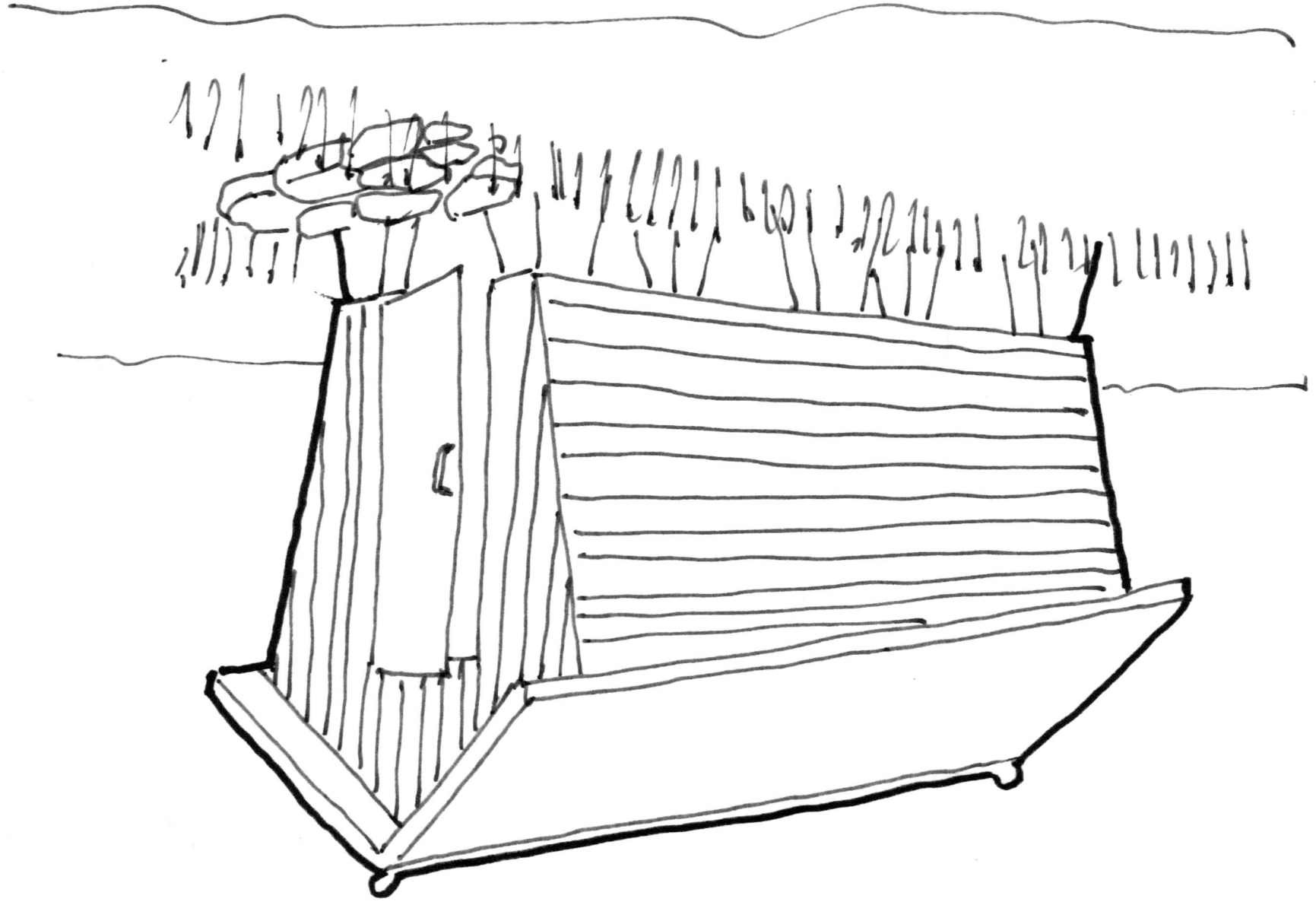

This is a gambrel roofed bank barn with a tiny corncrib.

This big barn in Cottage Grove has been repurposed as an event center.

A huge old dairy barn up by Rush City.

The 'Scandinavian barn' or elongated half log barn in Chisago County had cribbed timbers for cows on one side and vertical boards spaced apart for hay storage on the other. Smaller doors for cows, larger doors for hay wagon. It was used in the mid 1800s.

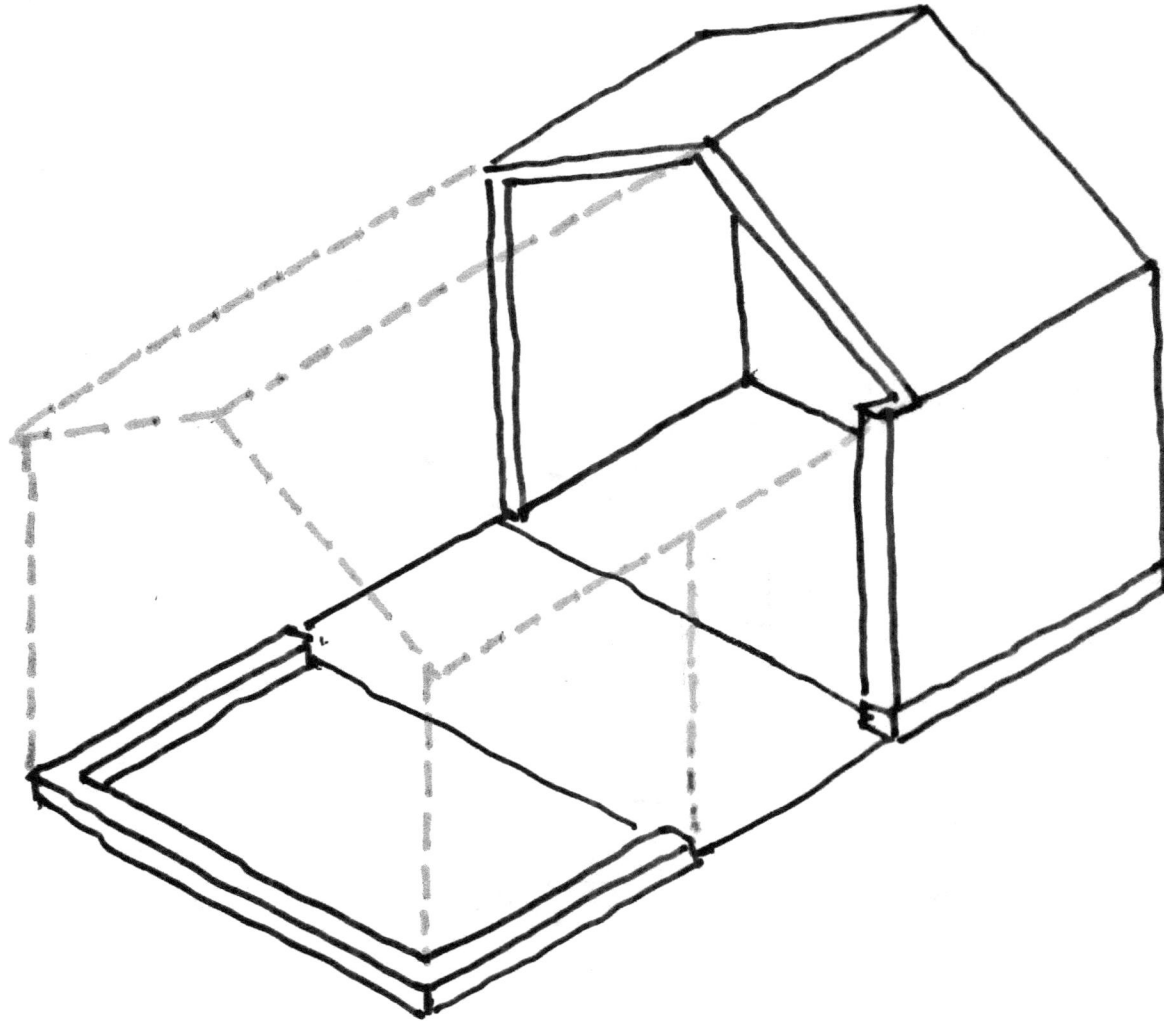

This is a diagram of a gable-ended, three-bay English Threshing Barn used by the early settlers.
The center bay was for threshing wheat and the side bays were for livestock or storage of grain or livestock.

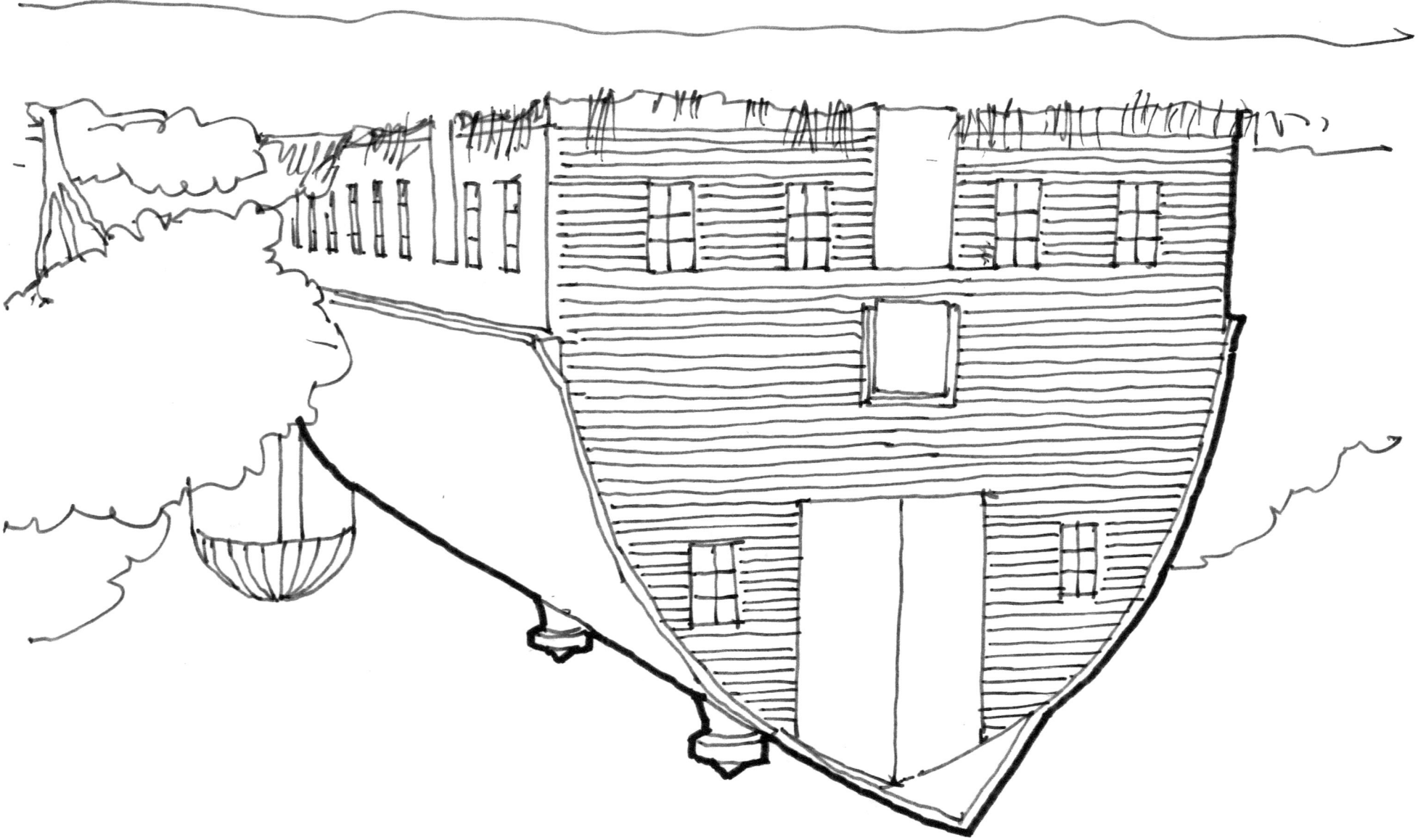

This barn is in Sherburne County and sports a gothic arch roof and horizontal siding.

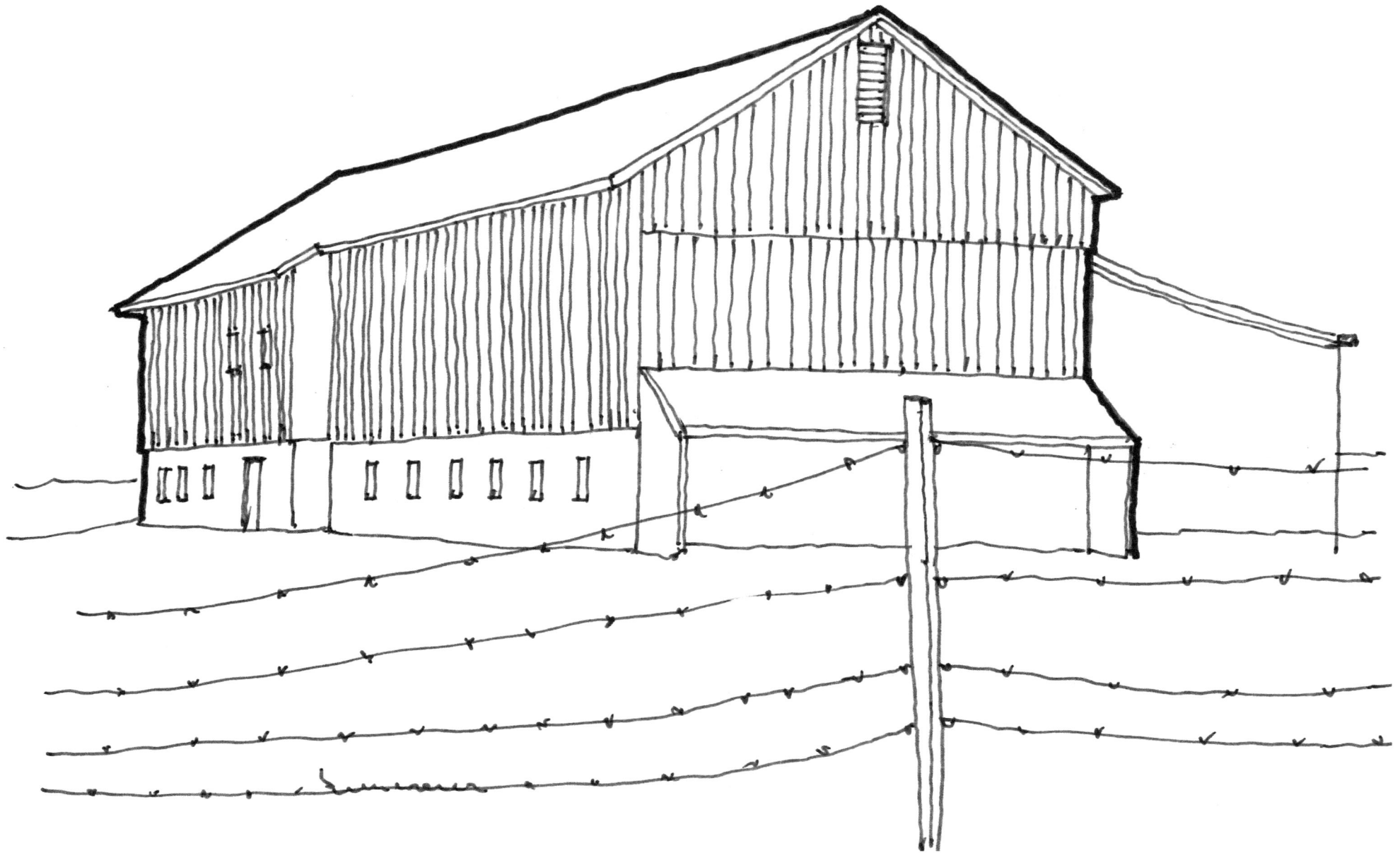

Here is a fine example of a gable ended barn with board and batten siding. There is a barb wire fence in front.

Here's a barn up near Harris built in the 1800s. Hay was stored in the big part on the left, cows were milked in the leanto on the right.

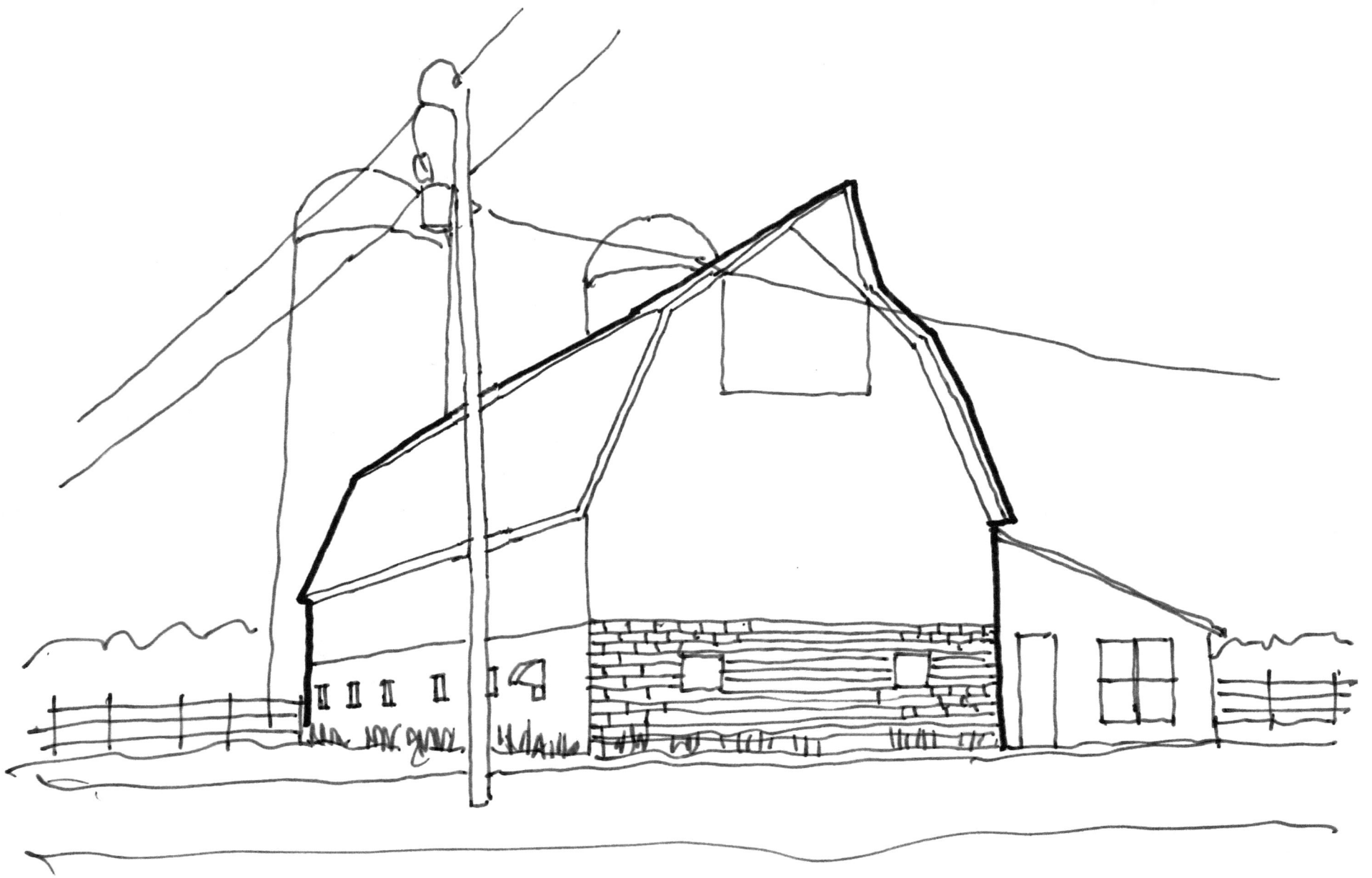

Dairy barn with a leanto, maybe a chicken coop.

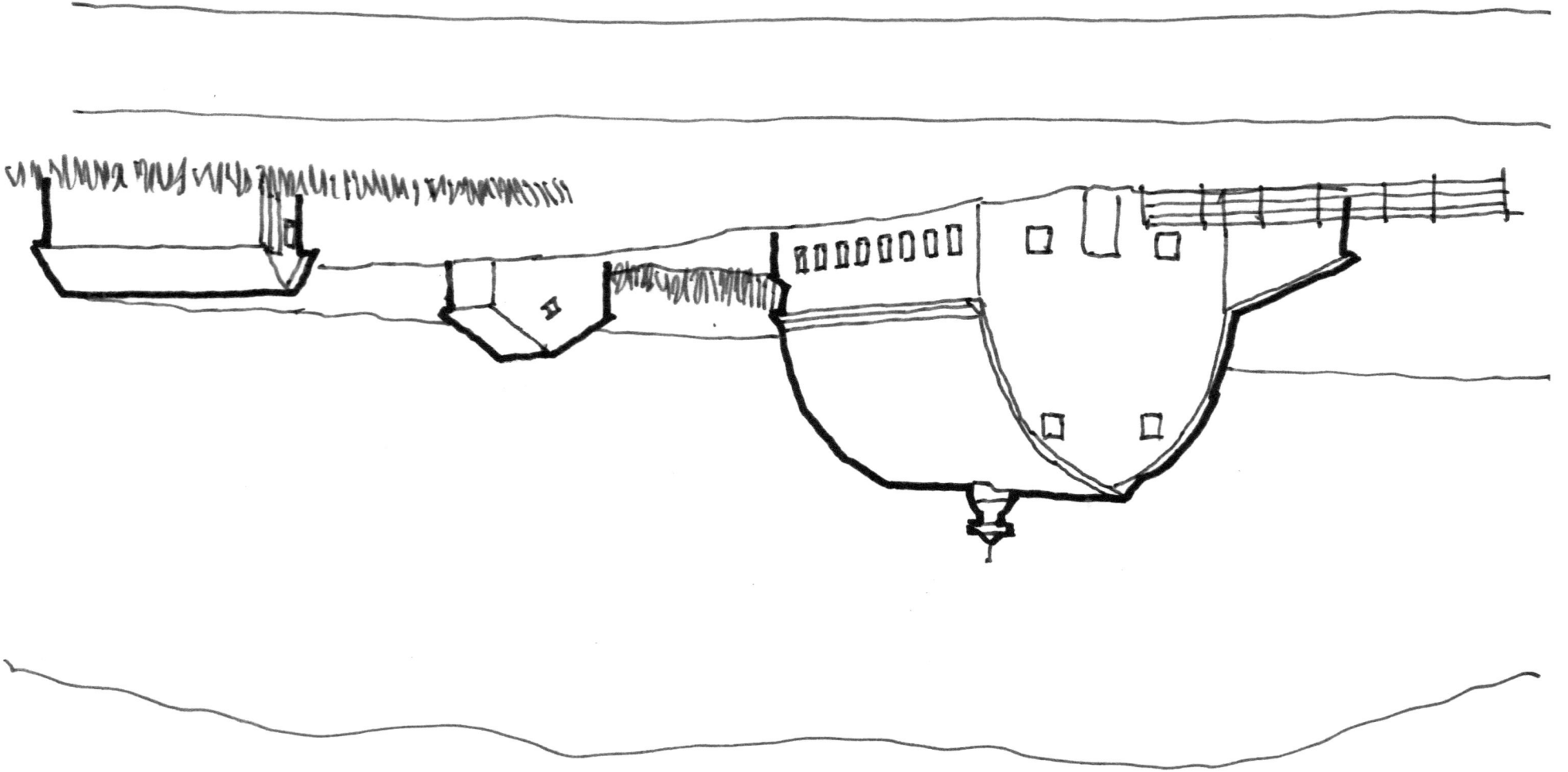

A big gothic arch dairy barn and friends.

This is a well preserved red gothic arch barn with white roof near Mankato, Minnesota.
It used to be a dairy barn full of cows.

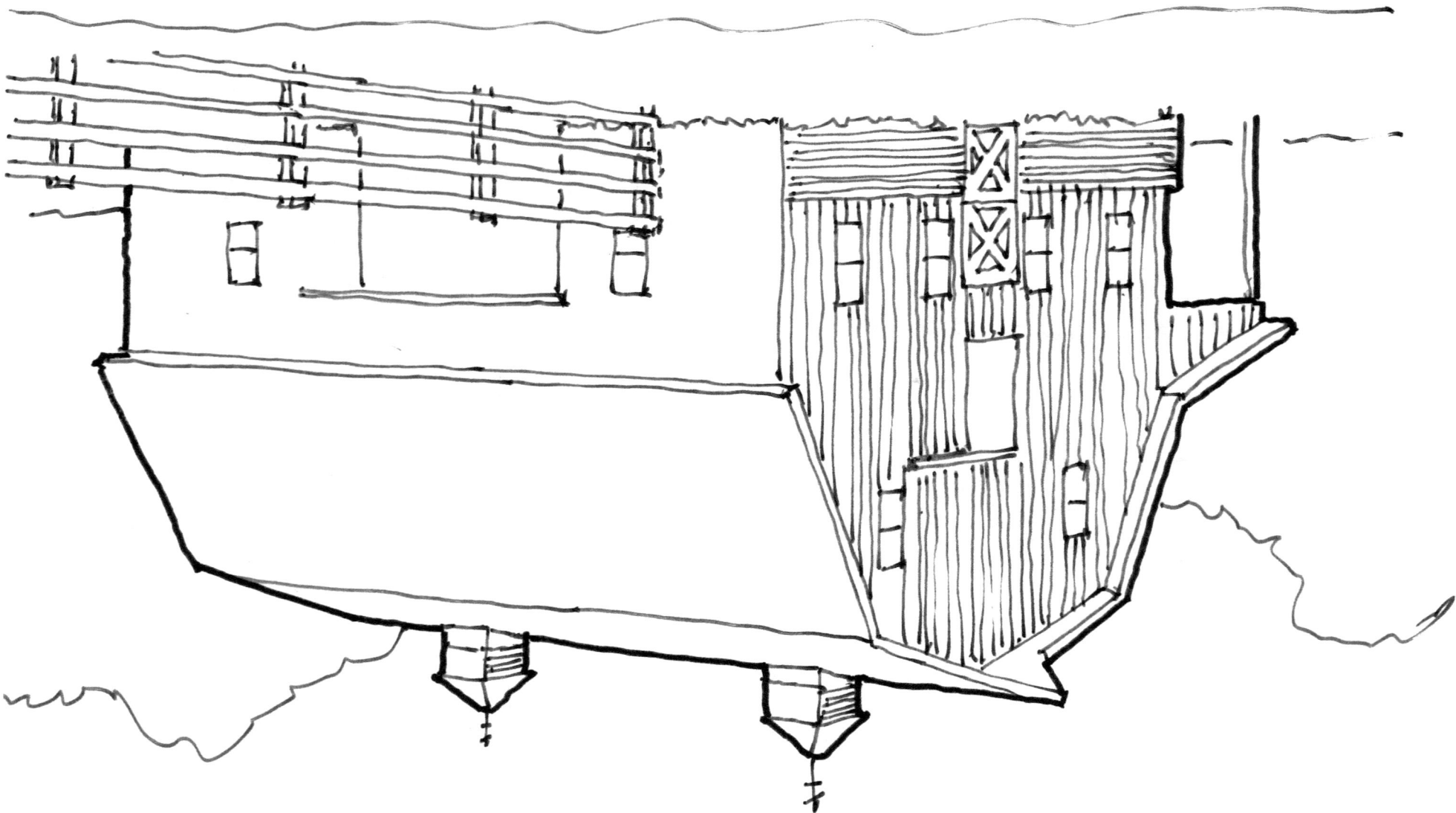

Nicely preserved gable-ended barn near Corvuso.

A very impressive barn near Scandia. It's L shaped.
Possibly to separate milk cows from horses and other cattle.

In this unusual 1910 barn in Washington County, the barn roof extends over the silo.
There is a dormer above the silo for filling with chopped silage.

There's a lot going on in this picture. Gothic arch barn with attached milk house, elevator to take hay bales up into the haymow, combination granary and corn crib at the left, and three tall blue Harvestore silos for storing chopped feed for the beef cattle.

Another well preserved gable-ended barn with milkhouse addition. Near Anoka.

A whimsical wintertime sketch of an old swayback gable-ended barn with a Gambrel-ended addition near Center City.

These identical twin barns are located just west of Rush City.
Maybe they were built by two identical twin brothers.

This gothic arch barn near Waverly has weather vanes on the rooftop ventilators and a brick foundation. A horse peeks out from behind the fence.

PULLEY

HAY PEAK

MONORAIL

PULLEY

HAY
MOW FLOOR

HAY
FORK

PULLEY

This is a diagram showing how hay was loaded into the haymow. It was invented by William Louden in 1867. Loose hay was picked up by a hay fork and pulled up to the haymow door under the hay peak and then transferred to a monorail so it could be distributed in the haymow. Horses did all the work.

Here's a tall dairy barn in Pine County.

This is a large farm in Chisago County. Two barns, one with lightening rods, three silos, one big shed.

This barn is in Hennepin County not far from Minneapolis. It is a gable-ended barn with a hay peak at the left end and a fancy cupola on the roof.

This is the Mary Knoll Barn in Rochester; it's really a huge double barn. It was built in 1920 by the Sisters of Saint Francis.

North Star Farm in Lake Elmo. Three barns connected, three silos and one horse.

This is a really huge barn. It has three cupolas and five dormers.

This old gable-ended barn has a lot of character, even old wagon wheels on display.

A pair of barns, one with a fancy hay peak and one without. Tractor in the field.

A lovely old barn with gambrel roof. Corrugated galvanized sheet metal siding and roofing. A splendid barn quilt.

A gothic arch roof on this 'bank barn' built into a hillside near Hugo. Cows enter the milking parlor on the backside. Notice hay peak on the left end, dormer roof over the haymow doors, and a small door in the big haymow doors. There's a circular barn quilt on the right end of the barn above the milkhouse.

This is a good example of a 'bank barn.' It's built into a hillside like a house with a walk-out basement. Cows below and hay stored above in the haymow.

This is what's known as a 'basement barn.' It has a first story on grade for milking cows and a haymow on the upper level with an earth ramp for the hay wagon. Near Stillwater.

This barn has not been used for a long time, but it stands as a monument to the farm that it once served. The silo has lost its roof. The small building in front may have been a small chicken coop. Near Scandia.

A conglomerate of farm buildings. Granary, maybe a chicken coop, barn and silo, and a windmill in the background.

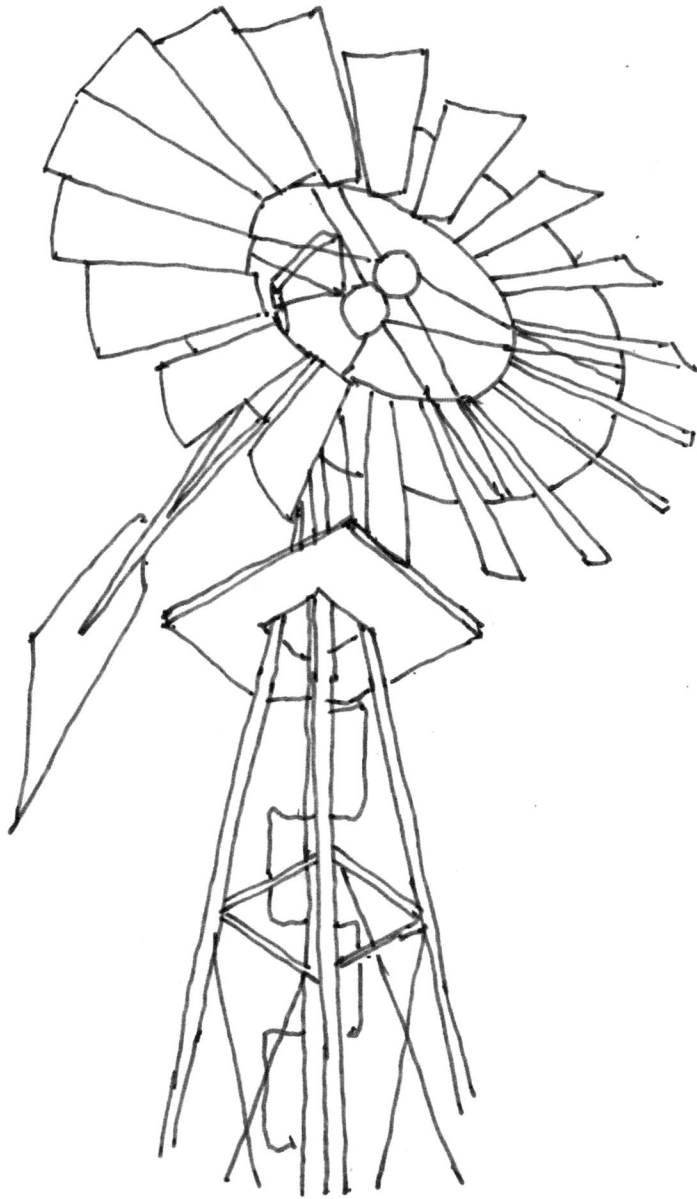

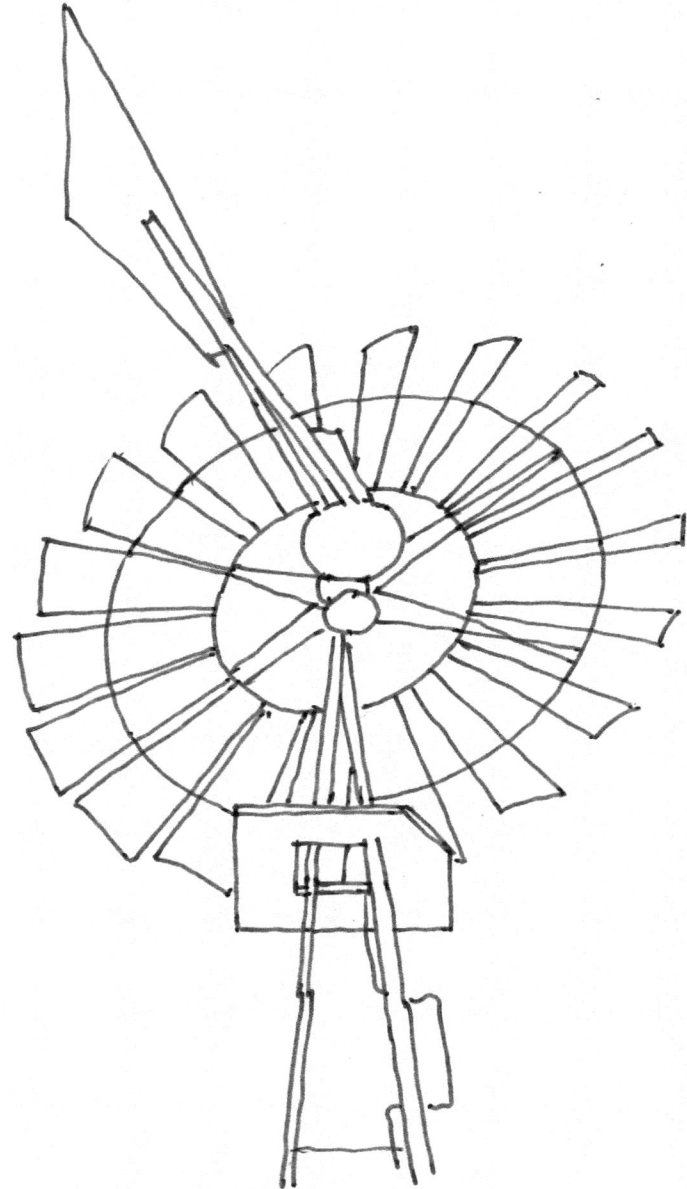

Here's a front and back view of a windmill. Before electricity came to farms, windmills generated enough electricity to pump water from the well.

This is a two-story round barn. Hay stored above, cows below. It is located near Rogers.

Built in 1915 into a hillside, Charles Moody's round barn is a prominent symbol of Chisago County's dairy farming industry. It is on the National Register of Historic Places.

A dairy barn with a brick foundation, a silo and a corn crib at the left.

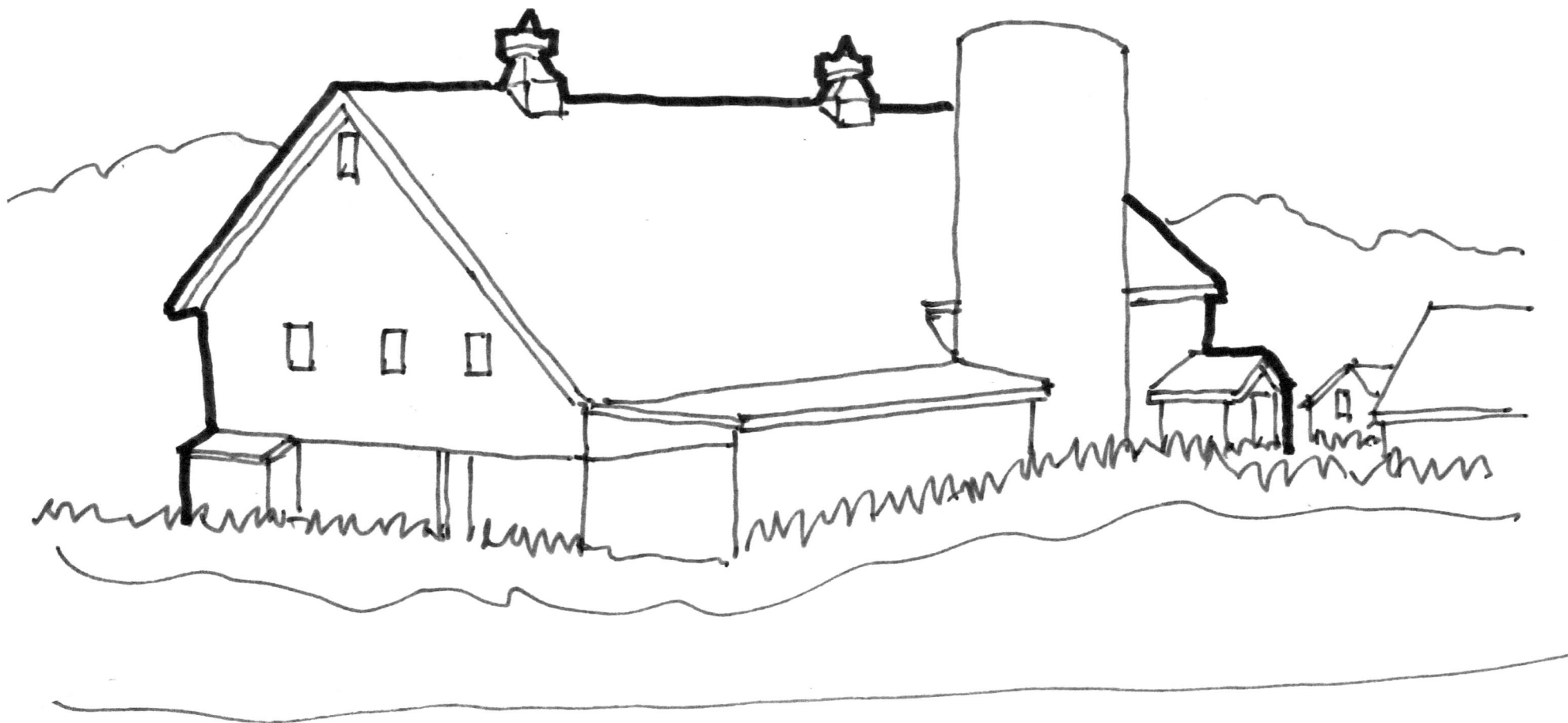

This is a unique barn roof—longer on the right side—and an attached shed and milk house.
It's on Quinlan Avenue south of Center City.

Coulter

Moldboard

This is a plow invented by John Deere for cutting through heavy clay soil.

Here's an old barn with a gable roof. The new barn over the hill has a gothic arch roof and a tall silo.

A well preserved gable-ended barn and a silo with a concrete roof located near Elk River.

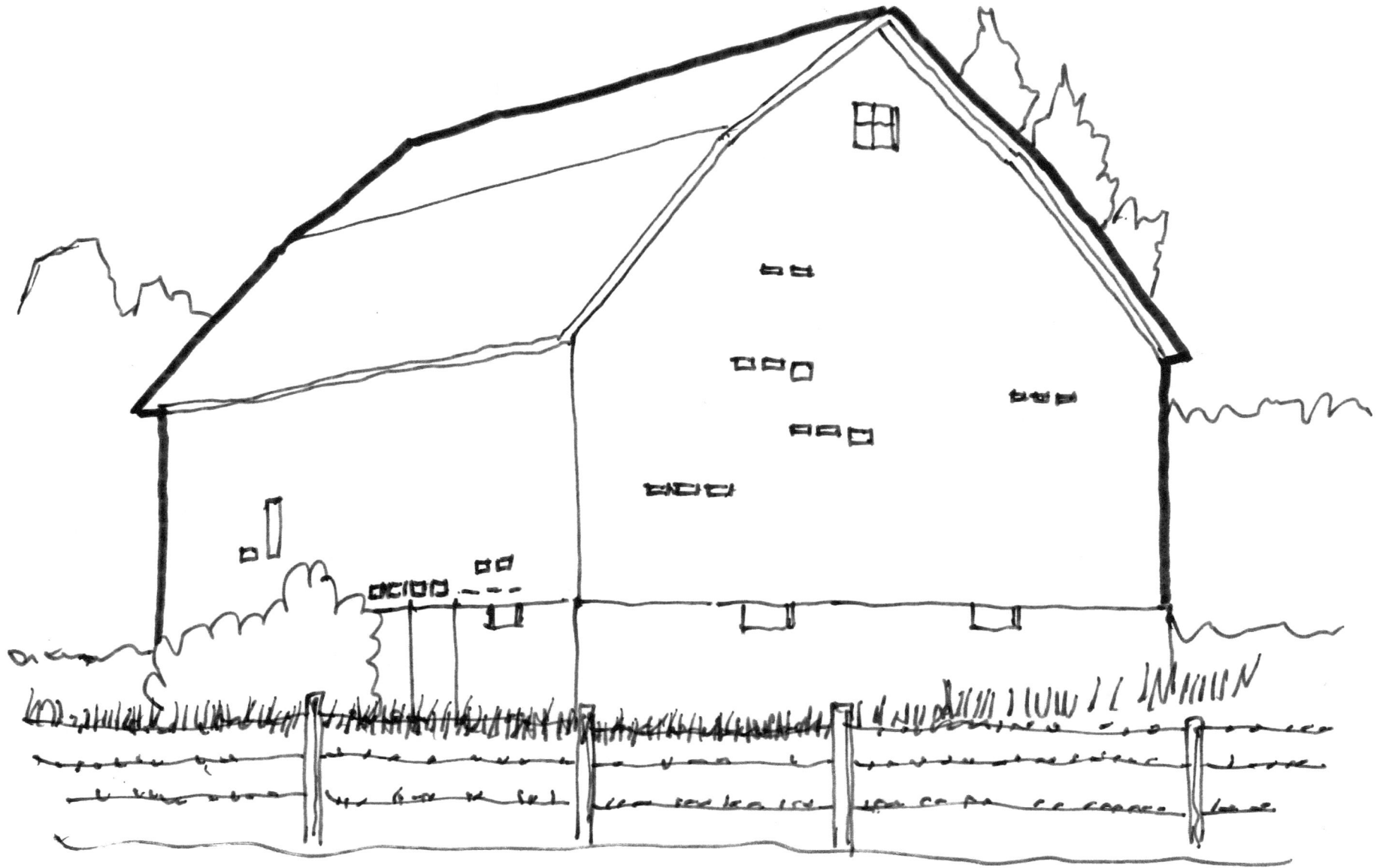

This barn near Willow River has a gambrel roof but it almost looks like a gable roof.
Where the horizontal siding is missing there are holes in the wall.

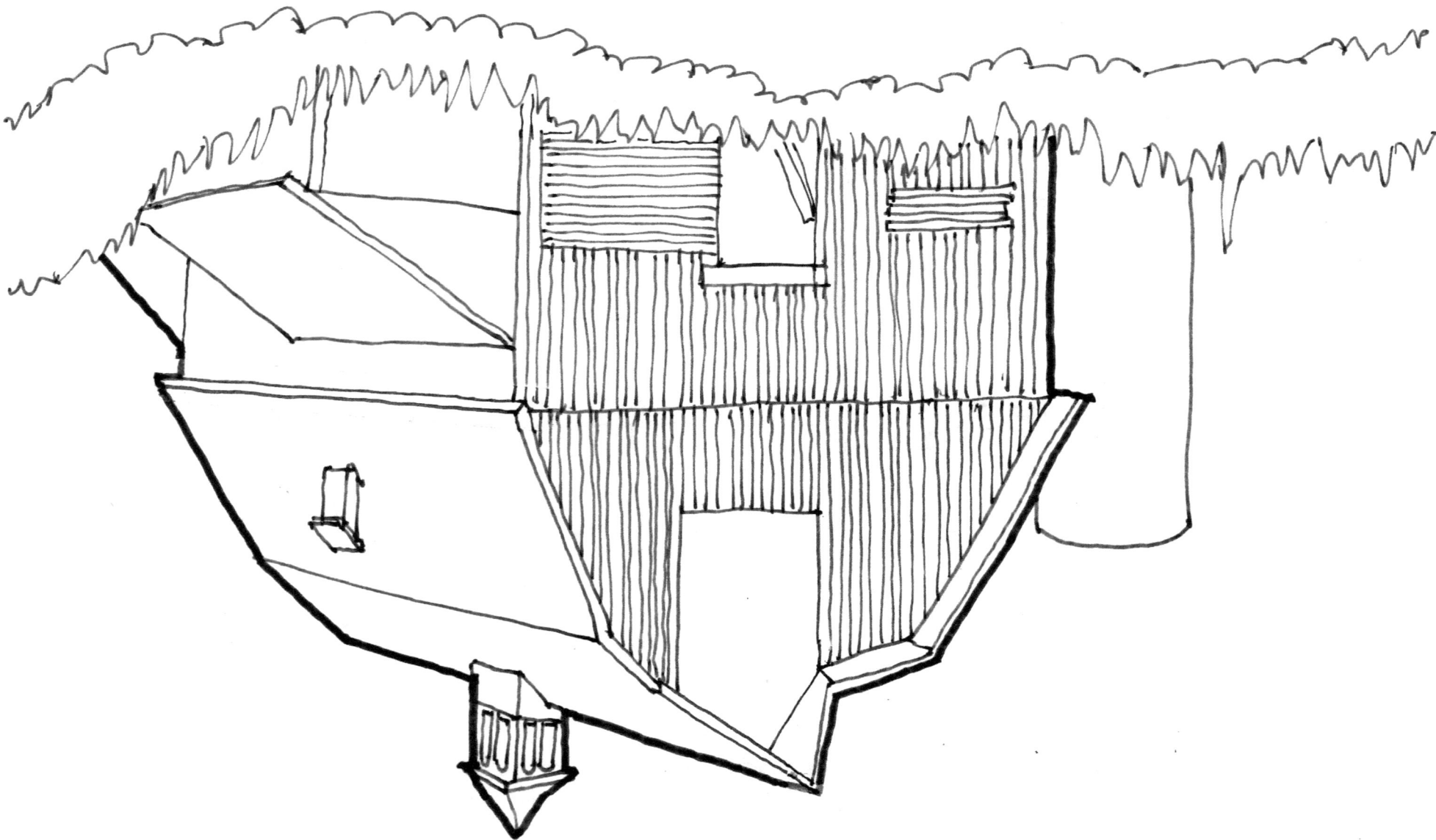

Verner Moller built this barn near Lindstrom in the late 1800s. It is hand-framed using tree trunks along the outside wall. A single hand-built cupola vents the haymow and a chimney or flue vents the lower barn.

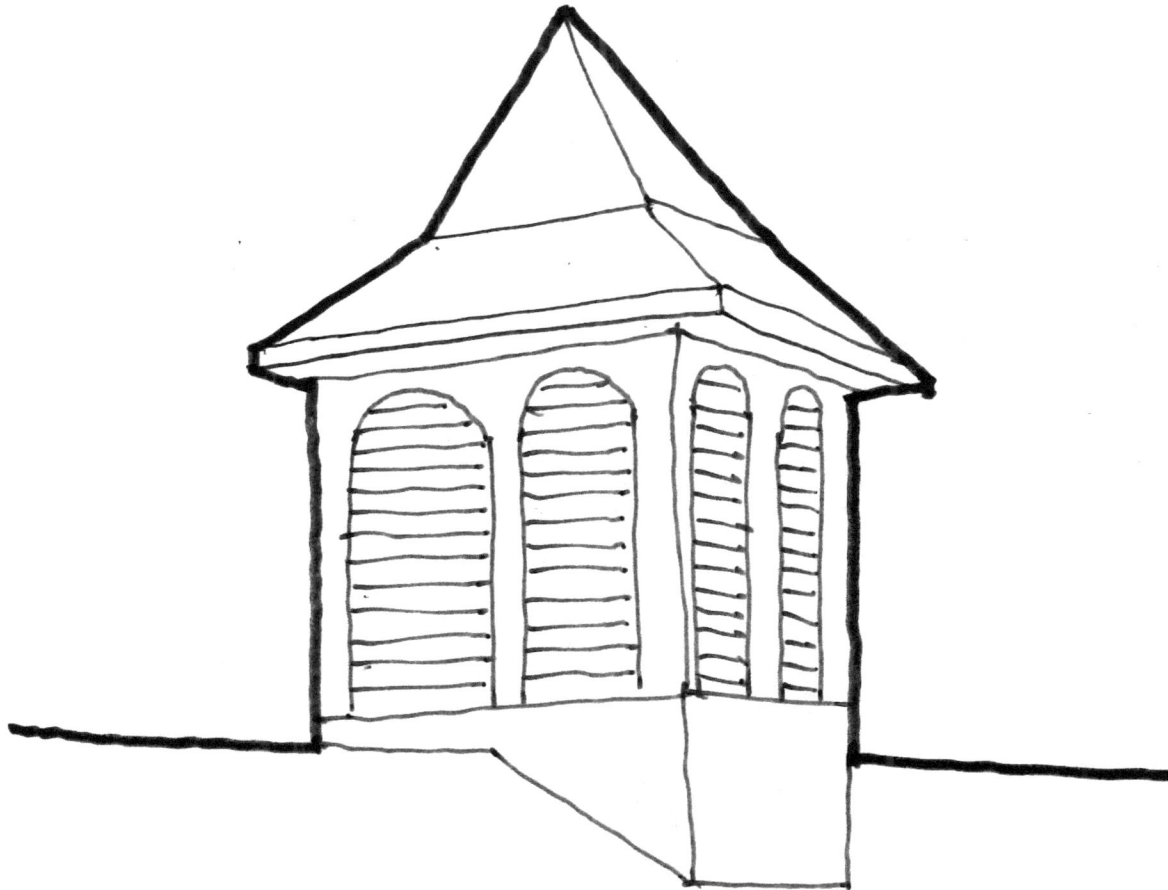

An enlargement of Verner Molner's Cupola.

Here's a rooftop ventilator, sometimes called a cupola. It ventilates the haymow so the hay can dry out.
Before the metal ventilator was invented, wooden cupolas were used.

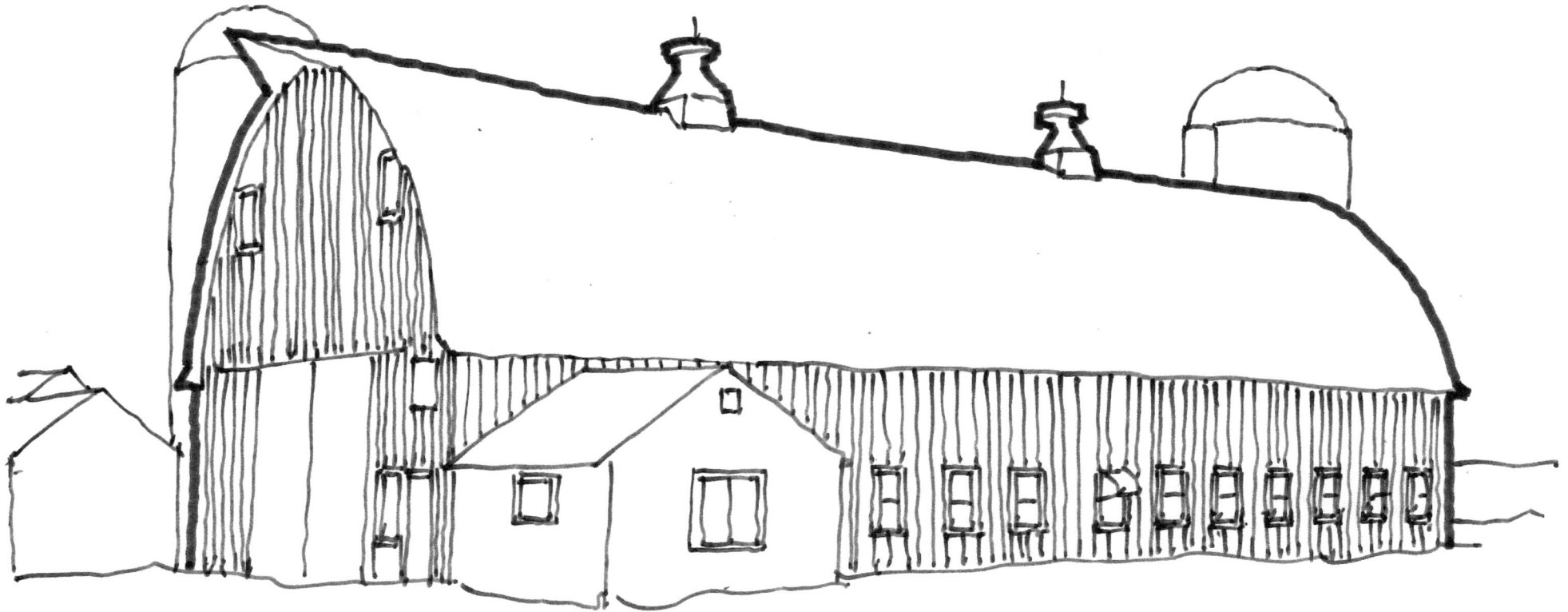

A simple gambrel-ended dairy barn with a trio of gable-ended out buildings near Kost.

This is the very well preserved and restored Lavander Farm. Here you see the pumphouse at the left, windmill and barn with silo. A few years ago it was voted the best farm in Isanti County.

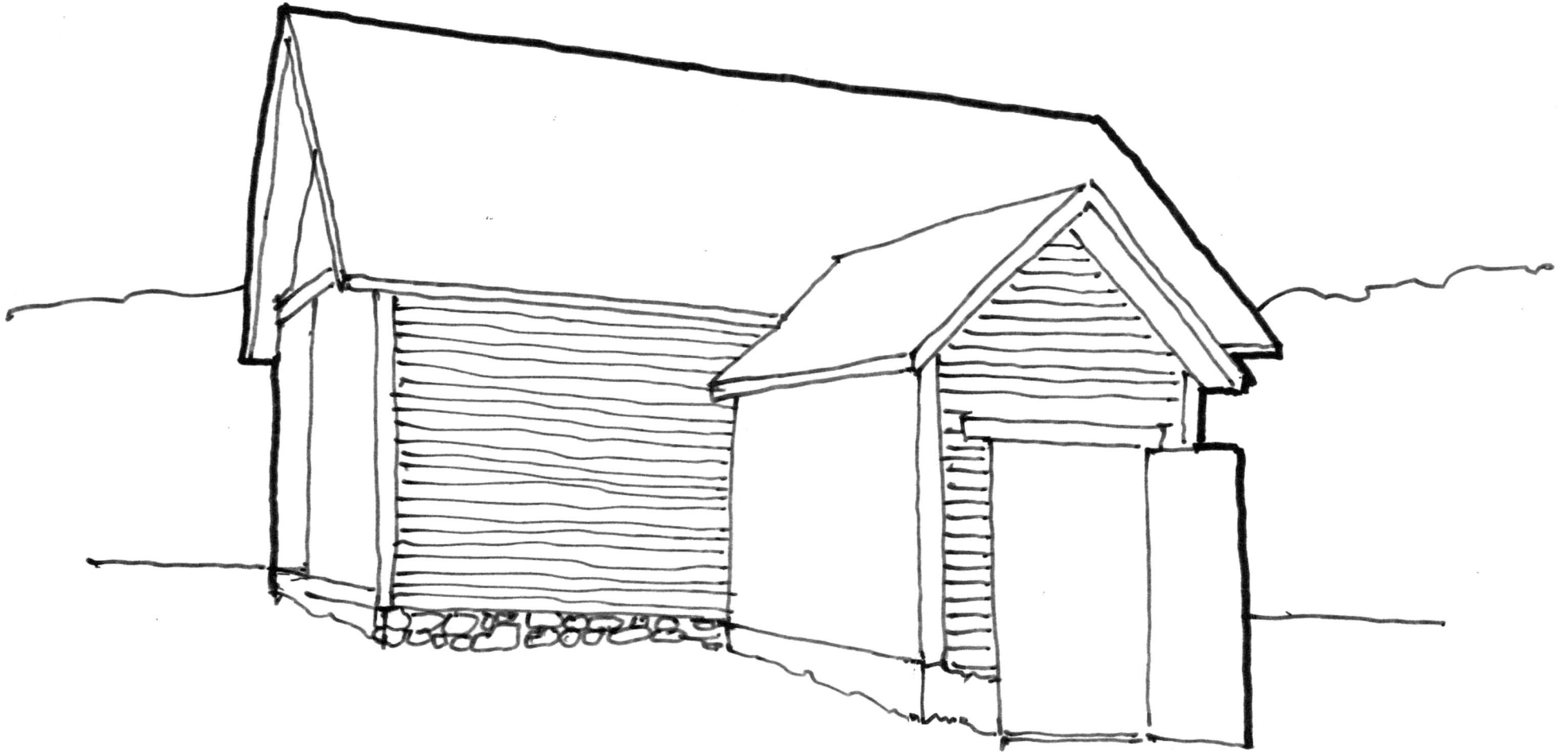

The door is open to a stairway leading down into the root cellar. Root vegetables such as carrots, rutabagas, and potatoes, were stored here over the winter back in the olden days.
It's part of the Lavander Farm in Isanti County.

Also by Jim Lammers:

Barns of the St Croix Valley: An Architect's Sketchbook
Capture the Moment: An Architect's Guide to Travel Sketching
How I Met Your Grandmother

CPSIA information can be obtained
at www.ICGtesting.com
Printed in the USA
BVHW02151414032323
660407BV00012B/908